A CHA CHAAN TENG THAT DOES NOT EXIST

一家不存在的茶餐廳

A CHA CHAAN TENG
THAT DOES NOT EXIST
一家不存在的茶餐廳

Selected Poems *of* DEREK CHUNG

鍾國強

Translated from Chinese by

May Huang

Zephyr Press

Published in 2023 by
Zephyr Press   www.zephyrpress.org

Chinese Copyright © 2023 Derek Chung (Chung Kwok-keung)
English Translation and Introduction Copyright
© 2023 May Huang

Cover image by Rita Gu

Author photo courtesy of the Hong Kong Arts
Development Council and Mr. So Photography

Book design by typeslowly
Printed in Michigan by Cushing Malloy

The Hong Kong Atlas is a series of contemporary writing
in English translation. Titles include poetry, prose, and graphic adaptions
from established and emerging Hong Kong authors.

We acknowledge with gratitude the financial support
of the Massachusetts Cultural Council and The Academy of American Poets
with funds from the Amazon Literary Partnership Poetry Fund.

Cataloguing-in publication data is available from the Library of Congress.

ISBN 978-1-938890-28-4

CONTENTS

ix   *Translator's Introduction* May Huang

2   鵝頸橋
Bowrington Bridge

4   筷
Chopsticks

6   蚊蚋
Mosquitoes

10   家務
Housework

16   雨餘中一座明亮的房子
In the Rain Stands a Bright House

20   地板
Floorboards

24   1:99
1:99

28   1 : 25000
1 : 25000

32   一家不存在的茶餐廳
A Cha Chaan Teng That Does Not Exist

36   福華街茶餐廳
The Cha Chaan Teng on Fortune Street

38   菠蘿包
Pineapple Bun

42   奶茶
Milk Tea

46   魚樹
Fish Tree

50   房子
The House

56   蝴蝶
Butterfly

60   水井
The Well

66   罐頭
The Can

70   節日
Festival

74   離傘
Umbrellonely

76   尋找一家麵包店
Searching for a Bakery

82   當我再看見河的時候
By the Time I Saw the River Again

86   燈籠
Lanterns

90   到了這個時候仍在寫詩
To Still Write Poetry

95   *Acknowledgments*
97   *Contributors*

Translator's Introduction

A cha chaan teng is a Hong Kong-style diner. Translated literally as "tea restaurant," cha chaan tengs are known for their fast service and affordable menu, drawing from Canto-western cuisine (a result of the British influence on Hong Kong culture following the Second World War). At a cha chaan teng, you can order Hong Kong-style french toast, rice served with char siu and vegetables, satay beef noodles topped with a fried egg, and other comfort food best enjoyed with milk tea or lemon tea.

Derek Chung begins his poem "The Can" by asking, "Why do I open this poem with a can?" I'll pose a similar question here: Why do I open this introduction by talking about cha chaan tengs? Because, although many cha chaan tengs (like the one in this book's title), have shuttered over the years due in part to Hong Kong's soaring rents, I want to resist talking about their "disappearance" (though this is a theme I thought much about in the early days of translating this book). While it is tempting, easy enough even, to talk about the things disappearing in Hong Kong today, cha chaan tengs are still very much present in the city, as is its active, literary culture.

Derek Chung's (Chung Kwok-keung's) poems have always reminded me of this truth. One of the most prolific authors in Hong Kong, he has authored eight poetry collections, three essay anthologies, two short story collections, and two books of poetry criticism. He is a frequent contributor to Hong Kong's literary journals and an active advocate of young Hong Kong writers. He is also an established translator, having translated Charles Simic, Li-young Lee, Williams Carlos Williams, and other contemporary English-language poets into Chinese. The various layers of Chung's literary life enter his work, which as a result incorporate different forms and styles; one gets the sense there's always a poem behind the poem. This collection brings together poems that capture the multidimensional quality of his work, spanning the last two decades, to portray a writer and city in-translation.

A central motif that captures this multiplicity is the house. In the poems, a house is never just a house—it's a site complicated by hope, constraint, and legacy. In "Milk Tea," the speaker as a child watches construction workers build his future house and feels a sense of wonderment; the sweetness of his tea seems to symbolize the sweet possibilities that the future house may bring. In "The House," sweetness gives way to the "stench of fish, meat, and exhaust fumes" as we come face to face with the reality of how difficult home ownership is in Hong Kong. Eight stanzas divide the house between its various owners, its space so compact that the speaker feels like a "snail" and can "practically shake" his neighbor's hand from the building next door. It is a poem that feels so personal, yet also manages to expose the communal, intergenerational problem that is Hong Kong's housing crisis.

Derek Chung is Hong Kong's "friendly neighborhood poet." His poems frequently breathe life into otherwise inanimate objects, imbuing them with meaning: in "Bowrington Bridge," we feel empathy for a scrap of paper soaring through the wind, whose hopeful arc through a busy city mirrors our own. In "The Can," a can of fried dace with salted black beans—a Hong Kong pantry staple—holds not only nourishment, but also the essence of mundane, yet sometimes magical, family life. In "Pineapple Bun," the humble bakery delicacy bears witness to the city's urban transformations, its delicate body juxtaposed against the callous outside world.

Though most of the poems in this collection were composed in the early 2000s, they also feel uncannily timely today—not because the world we live in hasn't changed, but perhaps because history continues to repeat itself. "1:99" is a "pandemic poem," written during the 2003 SARS outbreak, that captures the monotony and loneliness of pandemic times. The poem's mood is bleak; the repetitive sanitizing ("I use wet wipes to scrub clean all the handrails for the 221st time") and stench of a "long-worn face mask" feel all-too familiar today, as society continues to live with COVID-19. These images contribute to a stark sense of distance mirrored by the poem's title—the ratio 1:99, one man versus the masses.

Similarly, the most heart-wrenching poem in the book, "Housework," was written in 2004, the year the bird flu (H5N1 influenza) resurfaced in Hong Kong. The first outbreak of the virus in humans occurred in Hong Kong in 1997; in December of that year, the government ordered the slaughter of 1.3 million chickens to control the spread of the virus. This is the backdrop that informs the poem, which tracks how the speaker's relationship with chickens evolves from childhood to adulthood, and with it, his understanding of love and sacrifice. The speaker goes from addressing the chickens in his backyard:

> Was that love? I watched chicks slowly change their color
> Between rain or shine, I learned more about shifts in tense and tone

To ultimately addressing them in the context of the influenza:

> Is that love, for the children we removed you from the cookbook
> Is that love, for our own sake we piled up your bodies
> Like houses crowded together in the morning at night in a locked
>   down city

The repetition we see in "Housework" through the onomatopoeic "ah-ah" and the refrain of "is that love" is a common device that recurs throughout the work. Indeed, there's a degree of intensity, or perhaps tenacity, to his poems that is often reflected in the iterative formal structures. Even in a free-verse poem like "Floorboards," the stacked, spaced-out lines create a form of their own by resembling actual floorboards on the page. The dense poem takes on a physical weight, like its subject; "the floor never told / me just how much weight it can carry." When glancing at the poem, one gets the sense that there is almost too much to take in at once: which is the same sentiment shared by the poem's speaker, for whom never-ending chores and tensions in the family pile up like floorboards upon floorboards.

The intensity that characterizes the work takes shape most notably in his sestinas, two of which are included in this collection: "In the Rain Stands a Bright House" and "Fish Tree." In an essay he wrote about sestinas, accompanied by his own translation of Bishop's poem, Chung uses the word "tension" (張力) to describe the effect of the sestina's repetitive structure and layered meanings. The formal tensions created by the sestina structure amplify the emotional tensions already inherent in "In the Rain Stands a Bright House." The poem's emotional gut-punch comes from the tension between the sound of rain and the mother's silence; the weight of a bowl and the lightness of an empty table; the promise of ripe wampee fruits and the sadness of a sour fruit that only the bamboo sieve touches:

After mother returned, it was like she hadn't, making no sound.
The water in the well didn't ripple, streaks of rain didn't enter the house.
The rice cooker switched on, garlic filled the air. A wampee
falls out of the bamboo sieve, then unpeeled bites of unpitted days,
then fresh water, a trench, plates stacked on plates, a bed without
a dream.
It seems the steps we took have been retraced, adding no weight.

As a translator, there often comes a point in your work when you feel like you are not so much translating the text, but writing it, or living it. This is the feeling captured at the end of "Butterfly"—am I thinking of "someone far away / or myself"? I especially felt this way while translating the sestinas, sharing the poet's task of carrying six special words from one stanza to the next. Biking along the Shing Mun River last October, my first trip back home since the pandemic, I thought of "Festival," and the "paddles they lift on TV" that are as "neat as chopsticks." Sitting in the Berkeley Public Library on the first day of Lunar New Year, as Cantonese music hummed in the background, I began writing this introduction and thought about how I might as well be writing in the Hong Kong Public Library, one of my favorite places in the world (also where the author and I last met to discuss these poems).

Which brings me to the book's titular poem—"A Cha Chaan Teng That Does Not Exist." The poem was written in 2000 about a cha chaan teng that Chung frequented in the '80s, and is permeated by a sense of rapid transformation and disappearance; sounds vanish, words dissolve, railings are "suddenly torn down." The fact that he remembers the diner at all, the author muses, is because it shared its name with a coffin store— an ironic image that heightens the poem's sense of loss. And yet, what the poem shows is that by naming things, whether it be a pineapple bun or flock of chickens, by giving them space on a page, they live on in our collective imagination.

The cha chaan teng in these poems may no longer exist, but it certainly does here. So—pull up a chair, make yourself at home, and I hope you'll find Derek Chung, myself, and perhaps a little bit of your-self in this collection.

—*May Huang*

A CHA CHAAN TENG THAT DOES NOT EXIST

一家不存在的茶餐廳

鵝頸橋

一張紙在馬路
沒被風捲去

它在黑鐵去水渠罩旁
閱讀塵埃，並讓塵埃閱讀

已沒承載甚麼，撕下的一邊
看來也沒有隱隱作痛

不再是黑白的時事
或斑斕的廣告

汽車過時翻一個跟斗
巴士過時飛越行人道

打不著流浪的狗
打不著低頭走過的人

沒有名字在它身上
遇上了，誰也不會留意

鞋跟各各，也不會留意
打著一張飄起，又落下來的

紙，在路邊
等待竹帚，或另一次飛越

Bowrington Bridge

A piece of paper on the road
Isn't swept up by the wind

Next to a black iron drain cover
It reads dust, then is read by dust

Unable to bear anymore, a torn corner
Doesn't seem to be hurting

No longer the black and white of current events
Or a colorful advertisement

When cars pass it somersaults
When buses pass it flies over the sidewalk

Not hitting stray dogs
Not hitting people walking with their heads down

Without a name on its body
No one would notice if they looked

And the heels of shoes won't notice either
If they strike a floating, falling

Piece of paper, on the street
Waiting for a broom, or another chance to fly

筷

沒有誰理會抓出單數或雙數
昨晚，這只和那只配成了對

今午，它們都給遺棄在筒內
在一只一只孤獨的軀幹之間

沒有誰在意保存過去的記憶
每次進食前總是隨意地取出

多餘的穹窿一聲回到起點線
總有些落在讓人忘卻的邊緣

在日子的開闔間不斷地衰老

Chopsticks

No one cares if they grab an odd or even number
Last night, this one and that one became a pair

This afternoon, they were scattered in the tin
Standing between each and every lonely torso

No one cares about preserving memories
Drawn out at random before we eat

Extras are returned to the starting line with a clang
Though some always fall to forgotten edges

Aging in the opening and closing of days

蚊蚋

不知從哪時起我們不想母親操勞
逢年過節便到附近的酒樓吃飯

所以留在老屋的時間便比以前短
從四面八方湧來的蚊蚋便比往常兇

都像豁出去的樣子，成群蚊蚋飛到我可以
清楚看到牠們毛茸茸的觸鬚和空腹

的距

離

我不斷往空氣拍打，拍打。母親如常走過
間或跟我們閑話，渾然不覺滿屋是蚊

要起行了，母親。母親卻揉著肚子出來
說不去了，燈火漸暗的臉，說剛拉過肚子

可能是因為，鬢上未染的髮腳露白，今天下午
吃了一些，早餐未吃完擱在那裏久了的米粉

為甚麼不溫熱呢為甚麼不用微波爐叮呢？
冬至夜母親一人留守在家，拒絕了我們

我看到漫天蚊蚋很慢很慢地落在老屋的牆上
櫥上、椅上、桌上、杯上、碗上、筷子上……

Mosquitoes

I don't know when we began dining at the nearby tea house
Not wanting to trouble mother on New Year's and other holidays

Until the time we spent in the old house grew shorter
And the mosquitoes swarming from all directions grew fiercer,

Forming a herd, ready to risk it all, flying so close I could
Clearly see the space between their fuzzy antennae and

Empty

Stomachs

I slap, slap the empty air without pause. Mother goes about
As usual or gossips with us, utterly indifferent to a house full of mosquitoes

Ready to set off, mother. But mother comes out massaging her belly
And says no, face dimmed by lamplight, her stomach upset

The undyed, white hair showing on her temples, perhaps because
This afternoon she ate some of the vermicelli left out since breakfast

Why didn't she warm it up why didn't she microwave it before taking a bite?
Mother stayed home the night of the winter solstice, refusing our company

I saw a sky of mosquitoes slowly, slowly land on the walls of the old house,
The kitchen counter, the chairs, the desks, the cups, the bowls, the chopsticks . . .

時間是牠們的了。父親在電話上說母親睡了
不用擔心，而我在西鐵快線上開始感到頭疼

好像回老屋一次便多一次蚊子侵進我的頭顱
高頻震動的薄翼刺穿一種遺忘了的痛

Time belongs to them, now. Over the phone, father says mother is asleep,
Don't worry, and my head starts to pound on the West Rail Line

As if I were in the old house with mosquitoes invading my skull over and over,
Thin wings quivering at high frequency, piercing through a pain I had forgotten

家務

喔喔的我從沒有聽懂你的語言
我提起一個掏空了腹腔的身體

那是愛嗎？我在黝暗的禾稈窩裏拾起一枚蛋
仍然溫暖，回頭便見你在柴木堆裏探出頭來
喔喔的，像要對我說一些怎也說不清楚的話

那是一個下著細雨的下午嗎？我做著好像永遠做不完的家課
抬頭便見你在園裏翻耙泥土，蓬起的翅膀下是三五小雞雛
怯怯地探頭，忽然急步躍出，爭相啄食你嘴裏的甚麼
我看著你頻頻點頭，在微雨裏，凝望小小翅膀抖掉閃亮的水珠

那是愛嗎？我看著雞雛慢慢變掉了顏色
下雨和晴天之間，我學懂更多時態和語氣的變換
看見勞累的母親突然動氣，向我掄起砧板上的菜刀
看見桌上擺了一碗熱氣騰騰的餐蛋公仔麵
待我吃了好去應付午後悶長的升中試

喔喔的你在尋找你的蛋嗎？我在找我的嗎？
空空的方格待要填上甚麼呢？我望向窗外
斜風細雨又見你翻耙濕潤的泥土，深深的
一個彷彿永無止境的窟窿，藏下你的希望我的
希望麼？我看見漫天降下熱騰騰的蛋
我的喉管哽著，筆下一個字也寫不出來

那是愛嗎？一個下著冷雨的冬天
我看見你挺高了喉管，頷下的羽毛還未飄落
便見你把鮮紅的血瘋狂注入奶白的瓷碗

Housework

Ah ah-ing, I have never understood your language
I picked up a body with an emptied belly

Was that love? From the depths of the nest I took an egg
Still warm. Turning around, I saw you stick your head out from the firewood,
Ah ah-ing, like you wanted to tell me something you could never explain

Was it an afternoon of fine rain? I was doing endless chores
When I saw you rake the soil, while a flock of chicks beneath your wings
Looked around nervously, leapt, fought over something in your mouth
I watched you nod in the rain, gaze at glistening beads shaken by small wings

Was that love? I watched chicks slowly change their color
Between rain or shine, I learned more about shifts in tense and tone
Saw a weary mother grow irritated, brandish the kitchen knife
Saw piping hot spam and egg noodles on the table for me
So I could face the afternoon's tedious secondary school entrance exams

Ah ah-ing, were you looking for your eggs? Was I looking for mine?
How to fill in the empty grids? I looked out the window
At light wind and fine rain and saw you raking the wet mud, a deep
And almost never-ending cavity, hiding your hopes
And my hopes? I saw piping hot eggs descend from the sky
I felt a lump in my throat, and could not write a single word

Was that love? On a rainy winter's day
I watched you raise your throat, the feathers under your chin still intact
And saw you pour bright red blood into a milk-white porcelain bowl

來不及發出喔喔的聲音，你已躺在沸水盆邊
掏空了腹腔，瞪看自己一一鋪陳在地的內臟
然後在茫茫蒸氣中，你從一個白瓷盅裏升起
模糊了揭起蓋子的手，模糊了不斷增添的皺紋

而雨下了多時還在下我還在做我做不完的家務
下雨和晴天之間，我學懂更多簡單的方法解決複雜的問題
你有無端抑鬱的時刻，我學懂在旁靜靜地看
靜靜地洗瓶開奶，更換尿布，小小的搖鈴靜靜地搖
你有無端暴烈的時刻，我學懂吞吐言辭
收拾破碎，學懂在關鍵時刻，緊緊的從後緊緊抱著你
彷彿一對沉默厚重的翅膀，在漫天毛羽紛飛中
無有流血，無有掙扎，無有誰失聲委地

那是愛嗎？我買了一個九吋寬燉盅
內外洗淨，然後到市場買一隻母雞
隔著竹籠，我一眼便看到那異樣的眼神
沒有淚滴，只有那熟悉的，微微的
喔喔的聲音。然後寂滅。我看見血水
從溝渠流出。我看見肚腹
全掏空了。深深的，像一個口
甚麼話也說不出來。我揮一揮手
斷然拒絕店主手上閃亮的內臟

雨還在下水氣還在蒸騰我提起掏空腹腔的身體
喔喔的我好像聽到窗外傳來喔喔的聲音
我學懂水的份量蔥的性情火候的大小
端上飯桌的蒸氣準確盤旋在晴雨之間

With no time to cry ah-ah, you already lay by the hot water basin
Your stomach emptied, staring at your own scattered organs
Then in the vast steam, you rose from a porcelain pot
Blurring the hand that lifted the lid, blurring the ever-increasing wrinkles

It rains and rains and I am still finishing the never-ending housework
Between rain or shine, I learn simpler ways to solve complex problems
When you are gloomy for no reason, I learn to watch quietly from the side
Quietly clean the nursing bottle, change diapers, shake a small rattle
When you are angry for no reason, I learn to swallow my words
Clean up broken shards, squeeze you tightly from behind at key moments
Like a pair of silent heavy wings in a sky swirling with feathers
Without blood, without a struggle, without anyone losing their voice

Is that love? I bought a nine-inch wide steaming pot
Washed it thoroughly, then went to the store to buy a hen
Outside the bamboo cage, I saw that peculiar gaze
No tears, only that familiar, faint
Ah-ah. Then silence. I saw blood
Flow from a ditch. I saw a belly
Emptied out. Gaping like a mouth
That cannot say anything. I waved my hand
And refused the shimmering organs the shopkeeper held out

The rain keeps falling the steam keeps rising I pick up the body with
                    the emptied belly
Ah-ah, I almost hear an ah-ah from outside the window
I learn the water's volume the onion's temperament the size of the
                    cooking flame
The steam we bring onto the table spirals precisely between rain and shine

當黃油油的表層倒影臉上凝結的空氣
孩子又打噴嚏了是誰忘了添衣？
母親話來簡潔我聽到話筒那邊老房子的寂寞
春節回來麼元宵回來麼那麼中秋呢？
井水清冽風爐迸裂柴木還是去年的麼？
日子瘦得乾癟許是到了屠宰歡慶的時光

那是愛嗎？我看到你喉裏流著稀液如淚滴
那是流感麼我看見滿城的人拉長了面容
下雨和晴天之間，我學懂穿戴面罩和塑料保護衣
深深的翻耙泥土做那永遠做不完的工作
喔喔的我又聽到那聲音那聲音若斷若續
在一個一個飽滿的黑色塑料袋內密封了口
那是愛嗎為了孩子我們把你驅除出菜譜
那是愛嗎為了我們我們把你的軀體一一堆疊
像擁擠的房子在清晨在黑夜在關緊了的城市
我聽到那聲音那聲音就在不遠就在腳下
還未聽懂那語言便像日子般沉埋下去

When the oily yellow surface reflects the condensation on my face
A kid sneezes who once again forgot to layer up?
Mother's phone calls are brief I hear through the receiver that old house's
loneliness
Will you be back for New Year's for the Lantern Festival and what about
Mid-Autumn?
The well water is clear the tea stove cracked and is it still last year's firewood?
The days are shriveled thin, perhaps it's time to celebrate and slaughter

Is that love? I watch a thin fluid flow from your beak like tears
Is that the flu, I see an entire city of people with long faces
Between rain or shine, I learn to wear masks and hazmat suits
Deeply raking the mud, that never-ending work
Ah-ah, I hear again that voice stopping and starting
Mouths sealed in every stuffed black plastic bag
Is that love, for the children we removed you from the cookbook
Is that love, for our own sake we piled up your bodies
Like houses crowded together in the morning at night in a locked down city
I hear that voice that voice is at my feet
Not understanding it that language is buried like the days

雨餘中一座明亮的房子

——向畢曉普的六節詩致敬

雷聲最響的時候也沒有驚動樹上的黃皮
雨水溜過一顆一顆，在末端凝聚重量
然後在失神的一刻倏然墜落，好像日子
逐一碎散。母親抬頭，還是聽不到任何聲音
偶然提起右手，顫顫指劃眼前的房子
像要在早前歷歷的怖慄中，重塑一個夢

母親那時仍堅持說，床邊的黑衣人絕不是夢
蝙蝠即使顛倒了日夜，黃皮依然是黃皮
她要提防纍纍的記憶逐一遠離房子
於是為菜肴下更多的鹽，為碗碟添加重量
不斷往返園門，撿回碎石與落葉的聲音
鎖起來，像月曆上，一個一個圈著的日子

父親又再重述，母親年輕時待在家鄉的日子
柴在灶裏，棺在樑上，糙米蒸出夾縫中的夢
那時母親剛學曉寫姓名，來信，須旁人讀出聲音
然後滯留廣州，蟬鳴過後，樹上還是酸澀的黃皮
抓一把泥，雨水中也不知增添多少重量
然後是磚牆，古得發綠，孤獨也像家鄉的土房子

如今這裏的十三呎半，也層層疊疊得有若那房子
田地在下，禽畜在中，根與血相連的那些日子
疊加一桌桌菜肴與狼藉，以及人散後空桌的重量
「去，去，去！」父親偶然也轉述母親的開口夢
然後給雷聲隱去，樹上是連飢鳥也不再吃的黃皮
在雨水中，諦聽園門內外，也只有雨水的聲音

In the Rain Stands a Bright House

— a tribute to Elizabeth Bishop's sestina

Even the loudest thunder cannot shake the wampees
growing on the tree, where raindrops gather weight
and unexpectedly fall absent-mindedly like days
shattering in a row. Mother looks up but hears no sound,
abruptly raising a trembling right hand to draw a house,
as if hoping, amidst rising fear, to rebuild a dream.

Mother insists the man in black by her bed was not a dream;
even if bats invert night and day, the wampees are still wampees.
To stop memory's layers from gradually leaving the house,
she salts the vegetables even more, giving each bowl more weight,
and keeps returning to the garden to pick up the sound
of gravel and falling leaves, locking them up like circled calendar days.

Father recounts how wood burned in stoves back in mother's days,
coffins were placed on beams, steaming brown rice lifted dreams
from the cracks. Mother could only write her name, relying on the sound
of other voices to read. She stayed in Guangzhou, where sour wampees
grew even after the cicadas stopped singing. Grab some mud, its weight
a mystery, then a brick wall, aging green. Loneliness is our old brick house.

This thirteen and a half foot space is filling up like that house
in the field with poultry, with tables of dishes in disarray, days
connected by root and blood, and the deserted tables' empty weight.
"Go, go, go!" By chance, father repeats what mother utters in her dreams
then thunder swallows his voice, and on the trees are wampees
even vultures wouldn't eat. In the park, we hear only the rain's sound.

母親回來的時候，像沒有回來般不發任何聲音
水井的漣漪也沒動，雨痂也沒有走進房子
然後電飯煲按了掣，蒜出香，箕側翻出一顆黃皮
然後是沒有剝離的咀嚼，連皮帶肉的日子
然後是清水，渠溝，碗歸碗碟歸碟，一床無夢
離去的步履也像回來，沒有增添更多重量

雷聲最響的時候天空有沒有一定的重量
打在人間？抽屜突然打開了，沒有聲音
照片冊也打開了，人工的描色褪回黑白的夢
一襲一襲都是黑衣人，穿過衣櫃，揹起房子
揹起那些不易走過也已走過的日子
走遠，成一道灰色的山線，淡去，一如黃皮

「帶回去吧。」夢中母親捧出剛摘的飽滿的黃皮
聲音中有雨水的味道，風雷光影交相鬱積的日子
是要繼續承載那重量嗎？雨餘中一座明亮的房子

After mother returned, it was like she hadn't, making no sound.
The water in the well didn't ripple, streaks of rain didn't enter the house.
The rice cooker switched on, garlic filled the air. A wampee
falls out of the bamboo sieve, then unpeeled bites of unpitted days,
then fresh water, a trench, plates stacked on plates, a bed without a dream.
It seems the steps we took have been retraced, adding no weight.

When thunder is at its loudest, does the sky press a certain weight
onto the mortal world? The drawer opens suddenly without a sound,
the photo album flips open, sketches fade into grayscale dreams
of people in black who pass through the closet to bear up the house,
walking far away, becoming a gray mountain path that bears up the days
we managed with difficulty, fading away like wampees.

"Bring it back." In my dream, mother holds up ripe wampees
and the sound of her voice tastes like rain. Must the accumulated days
of lightning storms carry such weight? In the rain stands a bright house.

地板

你說浴室門要費好大氣力才能關牢　我便看見地板近門
的部分已發黑了　每夜回來在廊外便聽見你煩躁的聲音
兒子功課帶了回家？　在乾爛的飯粒與石子間我未回咀
甚麼帶了回家？　似無還有那骨刺又在某沿桌墜落　地板從未告
嚼　我俯身察看發黑的部分如何蔓
訴我可以承受的重量　房子瞪下的空間　霉黑的地
延　你又在面膜之後打量　老化的玻璃膠仍黏附舊日的創
板拱離原來的位置　我移開新疊的雜物
口　你又說找不到要找的東西了　女兒赤足在狹窄的走廊奔跑　我說拖鞋
像把話支開
呢拖鞋呢當心細嫩的腳掌　撬開門檻才看到裏面濕濡
的水漬　霉壞的部分猶如去年遺棄的蛋糕　你又埋怨
我甚麼也不願你看丟掉　我記不起已然丟掉的東西　起
皺的牆紙像你老看不完它的小說　沾濕不起的地方我猜測它化
開的文字　我沿牆搜索滲水的源頭　蒼白的瓷磚一臉無
革的樣子　剛要吐出的話語又沉沉回返　舌頭的裂紋
彷彿與日俱增　我把瓷磚表面抹得一滴不餘　關掉牆
裏日夜奔湧的聲音　你遙望窗外靜止的海　找尋照功
課怯怯改正的文字　防漏塗層散發濃烈的氣息　一室

Floorboards

you   say   it takes strength to shut the bathroom door   then I see the floor by the door has already blackened   every night I hear your exasperated sighs in the hall our son spreads out homework next to food that's no longer hot   what do I leave behind what do I bring home?   between shriveled grains and stones I chew back and forth   as if nothing happened bones fall silently down the side of the table   the floor never told me just how much weight it can carry   I stoop to check how far the black has spread behind a facial mask you size up the remaining space in the house   blackened floor boards arch away from their original place   aging glass glue sticks to former window wounds   you repeat you can't find what you are looking for   I move aside the new pile wanting to change the subject   our daughter runs barefoot in the narrow hallway   I say wear your slippers wear your slippers watch your tender soles   only after lifting the threshold do I see water stains   mold that looks like last year's abandoned cake   you grumble again that I never throw anything away   I no longer remember what I've thrown away   the wrinkled wallpaper is like the novel you never finish reading   I guess the damp parts are dissolved words   search along the wall for where the water began seeping   its pale tiles look so innocent   words I almost spat out return wearily   cracks on my tongue seem to increase every day   I wipe the tiles until they are spotless   turn off the rushing water we hear in the walls day and night   you look at the silent sea outside   I check the words timidly corrected on homework   the leaking seal emits a strong odor   a room of

舊物找不回昨日的味道　被褥覆疊新添的疑慮　夜色褪

忘記憶暗角的信箋　天花板不斷拓大的水痕給人看成倒

影　明晨你又會忘了自己的生日麼？　我猶努力把發脹

的霉木挖出　發現地板之下兀然悶響竟是另一層地板

old objects cannot retrieve yesterday's smell   bedding is overlaid with new doubts   night
forgets the old letters in memory's dark corners   the ceiling's expanding water marks become
shadows   tomorrow morning will you forget your birthday again?   I dig out the swelling
molded wood   and discover another silent layer of floorboards below the floorboards

1:99

當我是1，你是99

當我把稀釋的漂白水倒進浴室的U型去水位
當我第23次用酒精紙巾揩抹雙手
當我嘗試再用點力，擦掉杯沿咖啡或茶的陳漬
今早，牀腳下的灰，有一張收據

而幼腳蜘蛛大模大樣爬進相架背後露出便便大腹
給昨夜弄疲了的蜻蜓在光管下仰臥
我在網上第129次重看關於自己的信息
化名嘲諷，攻擊，然後矢口否認
自己是另一個自己很快便忘記的名字

當我拉開戴久了的口罩嗅到一股噁心的氣味
當我打開房子的頂蓋，警告上面一個也不認識的鄰居
當我開始學懂在骨碌碌的眼球中辨識新的符號
今早，電梯門打開，人群匆匆向兩邊的空氣稀釋

而一聲咳嗽可以免費換取身邊偌大的空間
維園一株樹木獨對躲開了的玻璃森林
我走過的路給自來水猛烈攻擊，電梯扶手
迎接盡頭塑料手套一團一團濡濡濕濕
圖書館緊急疏散前，我被一列一列靈魂拒絕

1:99

When I am 1, you are 99

When I pour diluted bleach into the bathroom's U-shaped trap
When I use wet wipes to rub my hands for the 23rd time
When I use more force to scrub coffee and tea-stained rims
This morning, in the dust at the foot of my bed, was a receipt

A lanky spider climbs behind the photo frame, showing its belly
Worn out from the night before, a dragonfly lays under the fluorescent lamp
I look myself up on the web for the 129th time
Making up a pseudonym to mock, attack, and then deny
I am another name I will soon forget

When I pull off a long-worn face mask and smell a foul odor
When I open the house's roof to warn upstairs neighbors that I do not know
When I begin to make out new signs with my rolling eyes
This morning, the elevator doors opened, crowds dispersed towards the air
on both sides

One cough can free up a large space beside you
A single tree in Victoria Park faces the hidden glass jungle
The streets I walk on are attacked by tap water, and the ends of
Escalator handrails meet the moist grip of plastic gloves
Before the library's emergency evacuation, I am rejected by rows and rows
of spirits

當我攤開地圖發現走過的地方從未走過
當我遮蓋眉眼露出下半臉的白色口罩
今早，當我揭開報章找尋醫院的新鮮數字
一隻僵固的蜉蝣正把蜘蛛驅逐出游絲

而我不敢開窗只得翻檢儲物櫃和抽屜
發現小津的秋刀魚塵封在希治閣的後窗
我問我們的結婚錄像要不要轉成光碟
你說你高聲地說誰看呢誰還看呢我說
甚麼甚麼隔著門廊走道隔著那麼多東西

當我用稀釋的漂白水洗過我們走過的地方
當我第221次用酒精抹盡所有扶手
當我取出萬能膠，嘗試黏回暴雨後霉脫的牆紙
今早，過期月結單內，有蟑螂乾屍

當你是1，而我是99

When I spread out a map and discover we never walked the places we walked
When I shield my eyes and reveal the white mask covering half of my face
This morning, when I opened the papers to find the hospital's freshest statistics
One stiff mayfly was driving a spider from its gossamer web

I dare not open the windows, so only look through cabinets and drawers
Discovering Ozu's *An Autumn Afternoon* covered in dust behind
                    Hitchcock's *Rear Window*
I ask whether we should turn our wedding cassettes into CDs
You say you loudly say who'll even watch them who's still watching I say
What, what, separated by the doorway, separated by so many things

When I use diluted bleach to wash the places we have walked
When I use wet wipes to scrub clean all the handrails for the 221st time
When I use universal glue to try fix the wallpaper that mildewed after the storm
This morning, inside the expired monthly statement, a dead cockroach

When you are 1, and I am 99

1：25000

我是雲我越飄越高你的存在縮成地面的一吋
你是紅色的超市扁平的旅館公園旁的P死巷裏的十
不管你變身是怎麼別安圖以小小的座標把我無邊的漫遊擊落

我是柱上刪塗的名字是帶血的鱗片是花圃旁歪倒的欄杆
白菜嫩瓣上水珠閃著八點鐘陽光慢慢滴落街角的陰溝
我在橋下仰望縫間的晴空等待改了道的巴士像等待洪水

我是風我是你想像的色彩是你當年草圖上勾勒的羽翼
二萬五千里在雪山在草原在鐵索橋上的挺進
我是星上午現的愛情是宇宙大爆炸裏不斷揮發的火星

我是街招上重複的號碼是網面單邊是無敵海景上葡萄的螞蟻
我用碎步擾亂麻雀的心神我用哀憐逐分丈量橋下的紙人
你的鞋跟落到天涯何處了我只記得我和你，走過的路不足一里

我是鳥我說過我是沒腳的麼我想我是只是不知腳有何用
若你真的用腳去證實二萬五千不過是一萬二千我想我會失笑
一拍翼我在漸高漸薄的空氣中回頭便忘記了底下的雲雨和色彩

I : 25000

I am a cloud that floats higher and higher your existence shrinks to an inch on the ground
You are a red supermarket a flat hotel the P by the park the + inside a dead end
Whatever shape you take don't bother shooting down my roaming with your minute coordinates

I am the names erased on a pillar the bloody scales of a fish the slanted railing by the flower bed
Droplets glisten on tender cabbage leaves the eight-o-clock sun drips slowly down the gutter
I am under the bridge looking at a clear sky between cracks waiting for the rerouted bus like waiting for a flood

I am the wind I am the colors you imagine the wings you sketched on the meadow that year
Twenty-five thousand miles pressing forward on grasslands on snowy mountains on torrents on suspension bridges
I am love suddenly found on a star cosmic dust vaporizing nonstop during the Big Bang

I am the recurring digits on street ads the only two shared walls the ants crawling on the best sea view
I disturb the minds of sparrows with quick steps I measure the paper people below the bridge with pity
Where on earth have your shoes fallen I only remember that you and I never walked a mile

I am a bird I have said I am a something without feet maybe I just don't know what to do with feet
If you use your feet to prove that twenty-five thousand is twelve thousand I may laugh in spite of myself
Flapping my wings I turn in the higher thinner air and forget the rain clouds and colors below

29

我是筵散後的杯盤是沒鎖鑰的鐵閘是入黑前的路燈
我在柱下等待冷氣機在頭上嘔囂塵埃在陽光裏枯竭
眉間我是一滴飲墜的髒水猶在想像洪水的擁抱和溫暖

I am the cutlery left after a feast the iron floodgate without a key the lamplight before darkness
I wait under the pillar the air conditioner makes a racket above my head dust dries up in the sun
Between eyebrows I am a dirty drop of water wanting to fall still imagining the flood's embrace and warmth

一家不存在的茶餐廳

我努力在記憶裏尋找你的位置
地磚上的花紋越來越模糊
腳影在還未熄滅的煙蒂間晃蕩
細碎的咀嚼聲音已在轉角消逝
我當如何確認某年某月
遺留在玻璃桌面上的茶迹呢
爐壁上關雲長的面頰
本是紅色，還是燭台的投影
或者根本就沒有關雲長
只有一些堆疊起來的壽星公
俯視微黃的單據浸入新沖的茶裏
我喜歡那種舊式瓷杯的厚度
邊沿一道道凹紋
彷彿藏著不同的故事
翻開肚皮串在一起的賬單
那迷惘的侍者已不知
從何說起
故事在他衣袋的上方
一印印原子筆迹上延續
化開來的地方
還有一些筆劃在堅持
玻璃門外有修路的標誌
欄杆漸漸圍攏過來
一日又忽然全部拆去
茶熱了涼，涼了用雙手溫著
話語隨腳步聲在門口推拉
沒有離去的選擇隱匿
在不為人注意的地方

A Cha Chaan Teng That Does Not Exist

I scour my memories for you
While patterns on the tiles grow blurrier
Shadows of feet sway between unextinguished cigarette butts
Discrete chewing sounds have vanished around the corner
How do I verify the month and year
Of the tea stains still on the glass table
Was the cheek of Emperor Guan on the furnace
Always red, or was that the candle's reflection
Or maybe there never was an Emperor
Only a few cans of Longevity piled together
Overlooking yellow receipts seeping into freshly brewed tea
I like the thickness of old-style porcelain cups
With indents lining the rims
As if concealing different stories
Flipping through a stack of bills skewered together
The confused waiter no longer knows
Where to begin
The stories sit above his apron pocket
As his handwriting spreads
And dissolves into his notebook
Still a few strokes persist
Road construction signs stand outside the glass door
Railings slowly circle around
Then one day are suddenly torn down
Tea is hot then cool, then warmed by our hands
Words and footsteps come and go from the door
Those who don't leave choose to lie low
In unnoticed places

就像你不響亮的名字
這麼多年以後
我應該不會
在混淆不清的連鎖名字中
記得你，如果你
並非跟那長生店同名

Just like your unlit name
After so many years
I don't suppose
That among the innumerable chain stores
I would have remembered you, if you
And that coffin shop didn't share a name

福華街茶餐廳

卡位直背而我總是
直不起背來
一個慵慵的下午
工作在遠方喊著寂寞
曾是午餐肉和煎蛋盤踞的飯丘
只剩幾顆油粒各自黯然
凍奶茶如常沿著吸管攀升
侍應飽溢頭油的稀髮卻頹塌下來
偶然的笑語，更多是望向門外
細聽小匙與瓷杯輕碰
光管如花奶瀉在茶裏的漩渦
早熟的餐牌為今晚的來客出神
牙籤的挑撥，不礙鹽在時間裏凝結
牆上的錢眼，對望一紙薄薄的早餐
糯米雞與咖啡，或茶
地拖橫掃時，零星的腳都習慣抬起
重回地面，還有一種踏實的感覺嗎？
感覺，像微涼的氹氳回歸冷氣槽
還是隨升騰的輕煙沒入
霍霍然廚房那具抽油煙機呢？
我捏著賬單邁向門口，想著
踏出門外是否還會想起
這個曾經那麼真實，那麼瑣碎的世界？

The Cha Chaan Teng on Fortune Street

Booth seats are straight-backed
But I can never sit up straight
On a lazy afternoon
Work cries loneliness from afar
What was once a mound of rice
Flanked by spam and a fried egg
Is now a few greasy, dejected grains
Milk tea climbs up the straw like always
But the waiter's grease-soaked hair falls flat
Making occasional jokes, more often looking out the door
Listening for the soft clink of spoon and cup
Fluorescent light streams
Into the tea's whirlpool like Carnation milk
The familiar menu charms tonight's guests
Battling toothpicks don't delay the congealing of salt
The tile on the wall eyes a thin sheet of breakfast
Lo mai gai and coffee, or tea
When the mop sweeps, scattered feet lift out of habit
And return to the ground. Is there still a sense of certainty?
Is this sense like a cool mist returning to the air conditioner
Or does it follow the rising smoke and disappear
Into the kitchen's ventilation?
I pinch the bill and stride to the door, wondering
After I step outside, will I still think of
This once so real, so trivial world?

菠蘿包

你是怎樣從童年走過來
街道都從寬敞走到瘦瘠了
玻璃趟門與起繭的手指角力
差點震掉你一塊表皮
金黃是碟緣昨日的茶漬
還是開業鏡面邊的鏽
你顫顫的居中默坐
思念如你的內在
一時沒有了內容

還是一直都沒有呢
不是的——
文字在牆上一直綿延
意義的盡頭還有一枚鈎釘
落單紙在等待一聲叫喚
破了兩個洞的桌布
以艱難的皺褶想望得更遠
而你鎮日坐在自己的山丘
看路的盡頭升起棚架
未夜陰影就移了過來
中宵你已立成了風露

還可以挺幾個朝陽呢
朝陽都躲到人面的背後
你躲進膠袋裏踏出街頭
膠袋也掛在你身上蹭到巷尾
一朝卸下來甚麼都不見
家當就是橋下鬱積的氣味

Pineapple Bun

How did you walk here from childhood
Even the wide streets have worn themselves thin
Calloused fingers fight the sliding glass door
Nearly shaking off a piece of your epidermis
Is the golden yellow yesterday's tea-stained plate
Or the rust on the mirror from opening day
You sit in the center quietly trembling
Wondering about your insides
Suddenly losing their contents

Perhaps there was never anything there
But no—
The writing on the wall remains
At the end of meaning a hook still hangs
The order sheet awaits a call
The two holes in the tablecloth
Use difficult creases to extend their longing
While you sit on your hilltop all day
Watching the end of the road hoist up scaffolding
By nightfall shadows shift over
Before midnight you are wind and dew

How many more sunrises can you endure
Sunrises now hide behind people's backs
You hide inside a plastic bag and step onto the street
The plastic hanging on your body grazes the alley
Once unloaded everything disappears
Family belongings are odors collecting below the bridge

還有文字倒寫至柱頂
給一下淒厲的車聲煞住

而你就像溢出的二氧化碳
在玻璃圍牆內尋找酵母
舊店只剩下了空殼
喚不醒曾經柔軟的麵糰
而你已化成仿古的美術字
像童年在灰濛的天空
倒放幻燈
顯影你一格一格的走回來
金黃變成蒼白
把身體剖開
只有一片靜待消融的牛油

While characters written in reverse on the column
Brake the sudden mournful wail of cars

And you are like carbon dioxide that's been released
Searching for the mother yeast within glass walls
The old shop is an empty hull
Unable to awaken once soft dough
And you have become commercial calligraphy
Like the slideshow from childhood
Projected onto the overcast sky
Showing you walking back square by square
Golden yellow turning pale white
Dissecting your body
A silent slab of butter
Waiting to melt

奶茶

母親用電爐燒了一鍋紅茶
便把半罐煉奶全澆在上面……

「歇一會」，母親像對篩沙的網說
蹲身築牆的師傅便停了手
磚刀、灰板、墨斗歪倒在牆下
師傅抬頭呵出一口蒸鬱的暑氣

母親說磚牆築得好不好
得靠一鍋好奶茶
有時是咖啡，有時是芝麻
糊得剛剛好，麥粥、番薯糖水
有時是煮得老爛的紅豆沙

有時奶茶面上漂著葉碎
師傅有時喝下，有時又把它
狠狠吐在篩沙的網上
影子晃動，靜止
半堵未批盪的牆
會是我們將來的房子

我把按照比例攪好的砂漿
小心放在師傅的身旁
看他們叨著煙，把磚頭逐一
堆疊，像一塊又一塊
威化，塗了過多的忌廉

Milk Tea

Mother brewed a pot of tea on the stove
Then poured in half a can of condensed milk

"Take a break," she said, as if to the sand screen
The craftsmen kneeling by the wall paused
Leaned trowel, slate, chalk line against the wall
Looked up and let out a sigh of summer heat

Mother says whether the tiles are built right
Depends on a pot of good tea
Sometimes it's coffee, other times sesame paste
Thickened just so, porridge, sweet potato soup
Sometimes it's red bean boiled to a pulp

Sometimes tea leaves floating on the surface
Are swallowed by the craftsmen, other times
Spit out harshly onto the sand screen
Shadows flicker and pause
The still unplastered half-wall
Will become our future house

We carefully place the mixed mortar
Next to the craftsmen
Watch them chew on cigarettes, slowly stack the
Tiles, like pieces and pieces of
Wafers, layered with so much cream

母親只顧收拾鍋爐和盆盌
我的口腔溢滿煉奶的甜味
都交予師傅了就像那奶茶
喝過了日頭西移水泥硬化
我們的房子就長出了兩肩

我好奇地用水平儀一量
氣泡晃了一會便停在中央
不偏不倚，如奶茶鍋裏
無人注意卻在那裏的泡沫

Mother only minds the pots and plates
My mouth is filled with the sweetness of condensed milk
It's all in the hands of the craftsmen now, like that milk tea
After we drink the sun moves west and cement hardens
Our house grows out two shoulders

I curiously measure the surface with a level
Its bubble sways then stops in the center
Impartial, like the foam in milk tea
That no one notices yet is there

魚樹

我們的日子是蒸在飯鍋裏的魚
只青葱仍在白霧裏尋它的顏色
飯顆無動，中午，僅傍晚記憶
就像餘光低至門檻趕及那影子
並讓夜如昨夜襲來，讓夜如水
流進你我的夢裏各開一株影樹

開一株讓沉默好好生長的影樹
花開花落，也沒驚動魚檔的魚
對面的菜販仍定時向蔬菜灑水
好讓你走過，更易察覺那顏色
只有陽光透明如小孩沒有影子
只微塵浮漾，那些，都是記憶

我們的鞋是否沾滿路上的記憶
太燦爛的都忘掉了，如那影樹
我們都寧願看腳下交錯的影子
在雨中消隱，那對鞋，像雙魚
相忘，交還一切可交還的顏色
可交還，如雨可以回天，如水

如水，已澄淨得一無餘波的水
苦瓜不再以深陷的皺紋為記憶
豆角的顏色，就是豆角的顏色
風雨無阻見證的，還有那影樹
見證了每條鹹魚的鹽均早於魚
比風還早風乾的，是它的影子

Fish Tree

Our days are rice cooker-steamed fish
Only green scallions search the white mist for its color
Unshifting grains of rice, noon, only evening's memories
Are like the last light chasing the door's shadow
Allowing night to attack like last night, allowing night like water
To flow into our dreams and plant in each a shadow tree

Plant a silence-nurturing shadow tree
Flowers bloom and wilt, not startling the fish stall's fish
The vendor splashes vegetables with water
So when you walk past, you notice their color
Only the sunlight, transparent as children, has no shadow
It is only floating dust, and those are all memories

Are our shoes stained with the street's memories?
The radiant ones are forgotten, like the shadow tree
We'd all rather look at our feet's crisscrossing shadows
Vanishing in the rain, that pair of shoes, like two fish
Forgetting each other, returning all the returnable colors
Returnable, like rain returning to the sky, like water

Like water, clear and rippleless water
The bittermelon no longer uses wrinkles as memories
The string bean's color is the string bean's color
Come rain or shine, still bearing witness is that shadow tree
Who testified that the salt on each salted fish came before the fish
Was air-dried before the air, and is its shadow

獨在水窪裏自娛的還是那影子
你想像黑夜的大海，鞋裏的水
倒出去年還未寄出的一雙鯉魚
加餐的飯桌還有否煙火的記憶
把夏天焚燒得睜不開眼的影樹
只縫隙透露那邊小郵局的顏色

屋邨又鬆上了另一俗艷的顏色
當年之將盡，最長的還是影子
還有那將日子六四切割的影樹
三五空碟，兩滴靜待蒸發的水
還藏有預知天寒的海水的記憶
遙向天邊，裂開，一肚白的魚

明天是餐桌上失落了顏色的魚
而影子也不再尋找影子的記憶
只有影樹，在夢中仍流溢如水

Entertaining itself alone in the swamp is still that shadow
You imagine the night sea, the shoe filled with water
Pouring out last year's unmailed pair of fish
Does the dinner table still keep the kitchen fumes in its memories?
Having burned so bright, summer couldn't open its eyes, the shadow tree
Only reveals through a gap the small post office's color

The housing estates are lacquered with a flashy new color
As the year comes to an end, the longest is still the shadow
And the tree that cuts days into several pieces, the shadow tree
A few empty plates, a couple silent drops of water
Wait to evaporate, holding the waves' winter weather memories
The distant horizon, split open, a white-bellied fish

Tomorrow is the dining table's colorless fish
And shadows no longer search for their own memories
Only the shadow tree in dreams overflows like water

房子

房子不是我的，是我父親的
雖然磚塊我有份製造
將水注入水泥混和沙和碎石
再倒進長一呎寬六吋的矩形木框裏
春實，壓平，慢慢移去木框
便是一個堅實的存在
升起十三呎半的高度，可以望遠
可以栽種玫瑰，延續新年過後的橘子
可以開四方的口，將風景納入牆壁
並沿樓梯一直滑下，停在地下一角的影子裏

房子不是我的，是房東顧生顧太的
不可以喧鬧，不可以有子女
不可以舉炊，不可以在燒水之外
燒其他甚麼。洗澡時用小小的面盆
把水潑上來，把濺在浴缸外的水抹得
一點痕跡也沒有。不可以夜歸
防盜鏈扣上，要勞煩顧生繫上睡褲出來
開門。房間不可以把窗擴闊，對面
重建成一幢彪形大廈，把影子蓋滿我全身

房子是我的，我把左手伸向一面牆
伸盡的右手中指便得暫時離開
另一面牆，約莫三吋光景。我放下百葉簾
把平日可以握手的鄰居排在外面。燃起煤氣
把魚腥肉臊連同廢氣盡情釋放
往外面想像裏遼闊得把握不住的空間

The House

The house is not mine, it's my father's,
Though I helped lay the bricks,
Pour water into cement, sand, gravel,
Into a wooden frame one foot long, six inches wide.
Pounding, pressing, slowly removing the frame,
We generated a solid existence
Thirteen and a half feet tall, where you can look ahead,
Plant roses, tend the new year's mandarins,
Open all the windows, allowing the view to enter the walls
And slide down the stairs, stopping at a shadowy corner on the ground.

The house is not mine, it's the landlord and landlady's,
We can't make loud noises, can't have children,
Can't cook rice, can't heat anything on the stove
Except for water. When showering, we use a tiny basin
For pouring, and mop spills around the tub
Until no trace is left. Don't come home late when the door
Is latched, troubling the landlord in his pajamas
To let you in. Don't leave any windows open,
A new burly high rise casts a shadow over my entire body.

The house is mine, I reach for a wall with my left hand and
The middle finger of my extended right hand leaves
The other wall for a moment, around three inches. I lower the blinds,
Shut out the neighbor whose hand I could practically shake. Light the gas,
Releasing the stench of fish, meat, and exhaust fumes
Into a space outside that is boundless beyond reach.

我一腳踏在客廳也是飯廳的柚木地板上一腳
踏在廚房暗紅色的方塊瓷磚上，感到踏實
感到電冰箱源源滲出的冷藏味道
在它投在地上漸漸膨脹的影子裏

房子是我的，在銀行誇飾的信箋
和地產代理頻繁更換的廣告之間
我感到房子的實在，就像蝸牛感到殼
敲下去有金屬的聲音。我慢慢走著
抬頭向前望去，感到金屬越來越輕
越來越輕，慢慢，向著膨脹的天空飄升

房子不是我的，是銀行的
我可以在屋裏多走幾步
好把想不透的事情想得透徹
可以望向遠方的島，望向更遠的海
想像將要來臨的無盡日子
可以望雲，望天氣的變幻
多寫幾首無關痛癢的詩
然後躺在更大更寬的床上
讓夢境擠出更多時間供我消磨

房子不是我的，是父親的
父親一次意外，從樓梯高處跌下來
跌在自己一手建造的陰影裏
甦醒後便開始繪畫房子的平面圖
藍色墨水像他眼圈未散的血塊
住市區的哥哥分了二樓半層
青馬大橋旁的弟弟分了地下一半
廚廁，客飯廳公用，而我分了
二樓另一半。我望著一絲不苟的

My foot in the living room is also the foot in the dining room;
Stepping on the dark red tiles of the kitchen, I feel sure-footed,
Feel the endless freezer smell coming from the fridge
In the swelling shadow it casts on the ground.

The house is mine, between the bank's enlarged letterhead
And the real estate agent's frequently changing ads,
I feel the house's certainty, just as a snail feels the metal sound
Of a knock on its shell. I walk slowly
Chin up, feeling the metal become lighter
And even lighter, slowly floating towards the swelling sky.

The house is not mine, it's the bank's,
I can walk a few more steps in the house
To clear the thoughts I cannot clear,
I can look at the faraway islands, at the farther sea,
Imagining the endless days to come,
I can look at clouds, at the weather transform,
Write a few more poems that have nothing to do with suffering,
Then lie on the larger, wider bed
To let dreams squeeze out more time to whittle away.

The house is not mine, it's my father's,
Father had an accident once, fell from the top of the stairs,
Fell on a shadow he built with his own hands.
When he woke he began sketching the floorplan of the house,
The ink was blue like the circles of blood clots under his eyes,
Older brother in the city gets half the first floor,
Younger brother by the Tsing Ma Bridge gets half the basement,
The kitchen and common spaces are shared, and I get
The other half of the first floor. I look at the meticulous

圖則，間隔和那些密密麻麻的
註明文字，漸漸回到我的過去
我的房間從那裏分出來，穿過籬笆
水井，爆竹碎屑和人煙，然後停在
不得不停的地方，那是甚麼地方呢？
我望著父親的眼睛，兩口深邃的井
分了的房子其實是一個房子

房子不是我的，父親和我都知道
我望著兩座島盡想著這些事情
兒子和女兒在身邊嬉玩
拉不動我便硬要我回答IQ題
如何用三刀將蛋糕切成八塊
我想房子將來，房子將來
是不是他們的呢？還是我和妻
付出所有後守著空闊的四壁
如平面圖上兩圈幽藍的墨漬？
「開估」，我沒怎麼想過就放棄了
兒子和女兒興奮地說出他們的答案

房子不是我的，我看著對面的島
遭一把刀子切成八塊

Sketches, spaces, and densely crowded
Annotations, and slowly return to my past;
I got my room from there, through the fence,
Wells, firecracker debris, and kitchen smoke, stopping
At the inevitable stopping place, what was it?
I look at my father's eyes, two deep wells,
The divided house is really one house.

The house is not mine, father and I know that,
I look at two islands and consider all this.
My son and daughter play beside me
They can't get me to budge so press me to answer an IQ question
How to divide one cake into eight pieces in three cuts,
I wonder about the future of the house, in the future
Will the house be theirs? Or will my wife and I
Invest all we have to guard four empty walls
Like the two dark blue ink stains on the floorplan?
"How?" I give up without really trying,
My son and daughter excitedly announce their answer.

The house is not mine, I look at the island
Cut into eight pieces with one knife.

蝴蝶

深夜回來
關門
便看見了
你
我背後的
影子
不斷拍
翼

該讓你
進來
麼？
手停在
門把上
一
秒

你在
門檻上
徘徊
拍打著
失神的
燈

一秒

Butterfly

got back late at night
shut the door
and saw
you
a shadow
behind my back
wings flapping non
stop

should I
let you
in?
hand paused
on the knob
one
second

you're
on the doorstep
wavering
flapping in the
absent-minded
light

one second

便平靜地
把你
寄入門縫

脫下
疲憊的
鞋
停止想念

遠方的人
或是我自己

then calmly
I slip you
through the door

remove
my weary
shoes
and stop longing for

someone far away
or myself

水井

那是老家瞪向天空的一隻眼睛
我親眼看見工人把泥從裏面掏出來
濕濕黃黃,黏黏纏纏,然後便有了水
從地層深處源源滲出,瞬間浸滿了
眼眶。我把木桶垂下,一把回聲
恍若恍若,迴旋著漣淪一圈一圈
向聚散的遊雲,說另一世界的話

那是桌上一杯水,靜止,陰沉
玻璃杯沿像井口的圍欄,我趨前
呼出的氣息轆轤而下,貼著苔綠的內壁
停在影子幢幢的水面。周遭沒有一絲風
但我感到水的清冷,沿我的內壁源源滲下
於是透明,看見底層微微挪動的物質

我在支流裏停止,兩旁新舊的樓房在蹲看
一輛巴士夾在前面的路口,交警的白手套揮舞
在黑壓壓蓄勢翻湧的頭顱之上,像無人注意的一絲浪花
身邊的人向天張大了口,沒有聲音,沒有手勢
文字像遠年的苔蘚,滲出古綠的顏色。我閱讀著
這城市的內壁,滑到最深最深的地方,又從那裏緩緩攀升

河水流動。壩下的水捲起了漩渦。黑色的水有白色的泡沫
我們在石上蹲著,用鎚子,有節奏地鎚打枯枝似的魚藤
滲出奶白色的汁液,流進底下錚錚鏦鏦的繁響裏
於是在堤岸不遠,我們看見仰向天空的魚肚白
像浮沉著的陰雲,偶然兩邊翻動,展示著死亡和希望

The Well

That was an eye staring at the sky in our old house
I saw with my own eyes workers digging out the mud
Damp, yellow, sticky, and filled with water
That spilled out from the depths, in a moment flooding
The eyelid. I lowered the wooden bucket, heard an echo
That seemed like ripples circling and
Speaking to clouds in a language from another world

That is a cup of water on the table, still, cloudy
The rim of the glass is like the well's railings, I lean and
My breath descends like a windlass, sticking to mossy inner walls,
Stopping in the water's flickering shadows. There isn't a wisp of wind
But I feel the water's chill flowing along my inner walls,
Becoming transparent, and see the faintly shifting substance below

I stop in the tributary, the new and old buildings on each side watch
A bus jammed in the crossing. The traffic cop's white glove dances
Above a surging throng of black hair like a wisp of foam everyone ignores
People gape at the sky without a sound, without a gesture
Words are like aged moss, oozing an ancient green color. I read
This city's inner walls, slide to the deepest, deepest place, and slowly climb up

The river moves. The tailwater turns into a whirlpool. Black waters froth white
We squat on rocks, using hammers to percussively strike poisonous vines
That ooze a milk-white sap, flowing into the clanking cacophony below
Near the embankment, we see white fish bellies face the sky
Like dark clouds, flipping over at random, symbolizing death and hope

我們擠過了瓶頸，三股支流匯成一道大河
有人用擴音器捕獵憤怒，有人在計算收成
有人張大了口，發出別人的聲音
河水越流越洶湧，陽光猛烈
直射河的最底層，沉著已久的淤泥和污砂
翻湧上升，邊緣閃著耀眼的光芒

我把一尾尾暈眩的魚撈起，放進河灘上的草簍
有些魚擱淺在石上，在草桿間掙扎翻身
我看著那些翕動的嘴巴，彷彿聽到牠們的聲音
在輪迴吐放的一個一個泡沫裏。我把一尾活像喝醉的魚
隔開，放進一隻盛著清水的小木桶裏
看牠勉力將肚子翻過來，如翻動一塊古遠的泥磚
一座搖搖欲墜的房子，一個被摺下的行囊
回家吃過鮮美的魚粥，吐著細細的
骨刺，便見牠在小木桶裏悠悠醒轉

河水流到下游，又迂迴分汊湧向四面八方的淺灘
有人傲立河岸，像口號不斷升高，在幢幢商廈間不斷回響
天空在窗洞裏默觀，堤壩在聲音裏顫抖，泡沫在爆破
我看到聲音，看到聲音裏面巨大的沉默，如一張一張魚的嘴巴

我想把魚放回河裏，但河裏也不是美好的所在
我想把魚放進瓦煲裏，但我們吃魚還不夠嗎?

河水的聲音在身後響起，在身邊響起，在身前響起
蓋過草桿旁的漪淪，石隙間的呼息，泥巴上的鱗屑

We squeeze past the bottleneck, three tributaries converge into one big river
Some use megaphones to decry hunting, some calculate the harvest,
Some open their mouths wide, letting out another's voice
The river surges on, the blazing sun
Shines on its depths, and the sludge and sand that sat for so long
Roll over and rise, their edges shimmering with dazzling rays

I dredge up each dazed fish, place them in bamboo baskets on the shore
Some are stranded on rocks, struggling and flipping in the grass
I look at their gasping mouths, like I can hear their voices
In each piece of foam being spat out over and over. I set aside a fish
The spitting image of a drunkard, place it in a pail filled with clear water,
Watch it struggle to flip its belly, as if flipping over an ancient brick
A house close to crumbling, a suitcase being set down
Returning home and eating delicious fish congee, spitting out thin
Bones, I see it slowly come around in the small wooden pail

The river flows downstream and meanders back to bifurcate the ford,
surging in all directions
Someone stands proudly on the bank, rising nonstop like a slogan, echoing
nonstop between dancing buildings
The sky ponders in the window, the dam trembles in the sound, foam
bursts and explodes
I see the sound, see the immense silence in the sound, like a fish's mouth

I want to return the fish to the river, but the river is not a place of beauty
I want to place the fish in the clay pot, but haven't we eaten enough fish?

The river resounds from behind, resounds from the side, resounds from in front
Covering the ripples by the grass, the breath between the rocks, the scales
in the mud,

簍筐裏的血絲。當河水染成氣球，岸上便有人宣告
聽，請聽，請聽河裏一把碩大無朋涵蓋一切的聲音

我雙手把魚捧到井口，向著一個深邃的影子
放下，然後靜靜聆聽，遠遠，一個，只屬於那魚的，回聲

我們都在發出聲音嗎？誰在聆聽？一道偉大行進的河
浩浩蕩蕩，沖激著堤岸，發出水井永遠發不出的聲音

我想像那魚，在老房子旁的水井裏，孤獨地轉悠身體
彷彿一隻鱗閃的眼睛，睜著魚肚白的天空

The blood in the baskets. When the river is dyed like a balloon, someone
on the bank declares
Listen, please listen, please listen to the river's all-encompassing sound

I use both hands to carry the fish to the well, place it down before a
Deep shadow, then listen, from afar, for one echo, that belongs to only that fish

Are we all making sounds? Who is listening? A great marching river,
Grand and mighty, rushes to the embankment, letting out a sound the well
could never make

I imagine that fish, in the well by the old house, turning over alone
Like a scaly eye staring at the fish belly-like sky

罐頭

為甚麼我以一個罐頭來開始這首詩呢？
那一個罐頭，當年開了便一直放著
我嗅到甚麼味道了呢？母親的手
慢慢伸到罐頭的邊緣，顫顫地，停住
讓日深的皺褶慢慢溶成桌面的紋理
我的家課，攤在一粒生僻漢字的眸裏

罐頭邊緣有血都成了痂吧，痂脫落在肉裏
讓味道變了而我們仍不知嗎？我們玩音樂椅
玩抓子，小布袋漏下微微發黃的米粒
讓佔不到椅子呆在那兒許久的拈來吃了
然後抿緊嘴巴，讓米粒在裏面轉悠，融化
像一個秘密，藏在我們都不知道的地方

母親習慣把要説的東西藏在罐頭裏
豆豉鯪魚的眼睛閃著慢慢收斂的油光
筍子翻過身又躺在原來的位置
肉回到鍋裏又回到同一個盛器
封密，還原，事物又重返金屬皮上的招紙
沒有撕開，我們會聽到字詞裏面的聲音嗎？

我們朗朗學成語，學現成的韻律和語法
父親下班後回來，回來了便一直忙
忙百合的開忙玫瑰的謝，氣息讓圍牆
收集層積慢慢壓成了桌，壓成了椅
讓我們團團坐著坐著便有了家的感覺
而父親，在我們朗讀聲中默默走進了泥土

The Can

Why do I open this poem with a can?
That year, the can was opened and then left out
What's that smell? Mother's hand
Reaches for the rim of the can, quivers, then stops
To let wrinkles slowly dissolve into the table's grain
My homework unfolds in the pupil of a rare character

Even blood on the rim of the can would now be a scab, peeling off in flesh
And changing the smell, though we still can't tell? We play musical chairs,
Play five stones, and yellowing grains of rice spill from a small sack,
Picked up and eaten by those who for ages could not get a chair,
Who tightly close their mouths, letting rice roll around inside, dissolving
Like a secret hidden somewhere we do not know

Mother is used to hiding what she wants to say inside the can
The eyes of fried dace in black-bean sauce glimmer and fade
Bamboo shoots flip over and lie down in their original places
Meat returns to the pot and returns to the same container
Sealed, restored, things go back to the labels on metal surfaces
If we never tear those labels, how will we hear the sounds inside their words?

We recite proverbs aloud, copy ready-made rhythms and grammar
Father comes home after work and keeps himself busy,
Busy with the blooming of lilies, the wilting of roses,
His breaths make the walls gather up slowly and fold into tables,
Fold into chairs so that we can sit together and feel at home
While father, to the sound of our recitations, steps quietly into the mud

那是風雨燭光中的一個罐頭
放了許多年仍一直放著
鉸碎了的肉暴露在空氣中
習慣了的氣味還會透露甚麼變化？
我們團團圍著，金屬閃著唯一的光源
照見昨夜的肉整合成為今日的午餐

為甚麼我以一個罐頭來結束這首詩呢？
那一個罐頭，現在停在超級市場的貨架裏
一個晴天，我為兒子讀出招紙上的文字
讀出一塊石，一灘泥，一場急疾的風雨
兒子並不明白罐頭和風雨的關係，看著我
像看著一個從未見過的，艱澀的漢字

The can withstood rainstorms and candlelight
It sat out for many years and is still sitting out
Chopped meat explodes in the air
When you get used to a smell, what changes does it reveal?
We gather round, and metal flashes our only light,
Shining on last night's meat as it's incorporated into today's lunch

Why do I close this poem with a can?
That can has come to rest on the supermarket shelf
One sunny day, I read out the words on its label for my son,
Read out a stone, a muddy shore, an urgent storm
My son did not understand the relationship between
The can and the storm, and looked at me
As if puzzling out an obscure character he had never seen before

節日

節日來了我們在門前踢球
狹窄的空間尚有兒子起腳的良機
我長於通坑渠，把皮球準確放在
樹與籬笆之間，一個角落
影子如常的黑

節日來了兒子跟表弟玩電腦
皇馬對英格蘭可以12比0
碧咸掃跌碧咸——Penalty! Penalty！
我在翻報章斗大的標題
戴墨鏡的地產商大義滅親
笑咪咪把昨天的自己摑落在報屁股下

節日來了我們吃肉
吐骨，把湯喝得呼呼作響
電視上舉起的木楫像筷子一樣齊
水花一樣高。我們喝掉所有青啤
眼睛跳進城門河洗掉去年的晦氣

節日來了我們摘樹上的黃皮
妻子說甜我說有點酸
沉色的才是成熟的呀妻說
我拿了一 把給兒子他說不想吃
我拿了一顆給女兒她掉頭便走了

Festival

The festival is here we play football by the door
Even in a tight space my son can nail a kickoff
Skilled at the nutmeg, I plan to place the ball
Between the tree and hedge, a corner
The shadows are dark as always

The festival is here my son games with cousins
Real Madrid versus England, the score is 12–0
Beckham fouls Beckham—Penalty! Penalty!
I flip the paper's looming headlines
The shady real estate agent holds law above family
Cackling, he slaps yesterday's self onto the paper's ass

The festival is here we eat meat
Spit bones, noisily slurp soup
The paddles they lift on TV are neat as chopsticks,
High as splashes. We down all the Tsingtao
And our eyes jump into the Shing Mun River
To rinse away last year's bad luck

The festival is here we pick wampee fruits
My wife says they're sweet I say sour
The darker ones are ripest she says
I bring a bunch to my son he says no
I bring one to my daughter she walks away

節日來了電視上有脅殺人質的消息
蒸氣升騰母親的湯越來越入味
父親說買來的雞須養一段時日才宰殺
糉子吃淡了我們的餐桌需要一點糖

節日來了我暫停問功課
兒子反問那人為何跳下去
我說或許，或許他要證明一些甚麼吧
但事實證明他還未學會游泳呀
對，這世代，要學好游泳便是這道理

節日來了我們難得胡謅
我們唱歌然後忘記歌詞
我們歡聚然後各自歸家
節日來了我們潛入海底隧道
慶幸還有引擎聲音
像波浪不斷為我們催眠

The festival is here news of murder is on TV
Steam rises and mother's soup turns tastier
Father says you must wait to slaughter chicken
After plain zongzi our table needs a little sugar

The festival is here I stop asking about homework
Yet my son asks why the man jumped in
I say perhaps, perhaps he had something to prove
Aha, but in truth he proved he could not swim
Yes, in today's age, this is why you learn to swim

The festival is here we get to talk nonsense
We sing and forget lyrics
We gather and go home
The festival is here we dive into the Cross-Harbor Tunnel
Thankful for the whir of engines
Hypnotizing us like waves

離傘

大雨過後不期然遇見你
當我在大廈入口整理半濕的衣衫
你卻在那邊的水池向我凝視
墨綠的外衣斜褪下來
露出屈折了的傘骨
彷彿還想在毛毛雨中垂釣
早已遠去了的故事
這故事甚麼時候開始的呢
如魚之於山泉
雨之於海洋
這時我已走在玻璃幕牆後
瞥見你從道旁的垃圾箱裏
探出頭來
彷彿雨停後怯怯伸出的掌心
而天空已沒有任何給予
廉價的塑料手柄
還在念掛最初的手溫嗎
雨真的停了
新傘如鰓合上
我打開辦公室的玻璃大門
如一尾魚游進
冷氣如水的空間

Umbrellonely

after the storm I did not expect to see you
as I arranged my damp clothes in the building
but there you were looking at me from the pond
your dark green coat slipped off slightly
showing the bent bones of an umbrella
as if in this drizzling rain you still wanted
to fish for stories long gone
when did this story begin
a fish is to the mountain spring
what rain is to the sea
I walked behind the glassy curtain wall
glimpsed your head in a nearby trash can
poking out
like a palm timidly extended after rain
yet the sky has nothing more to give
does a cheap plastic handle
still miss the first warm touch of a hand?
the rain has really stopped
new umbrellas close like gills
I open the glass door of the office
and swim like a fish
into an air conditioned sea

尋找一家麵包店

惺忪的巷弄應該無意
讓我多拐了幾個彎
這我是知道的
我知道陽光在前面不遠
雖然露台還未露面
或向我點頭示意
路上也沒有一個人
摘一片樹葉
無端停步
向頭上的街燈微笑

這我都知道
我知道這城有太多
水果酒和Tapas
就像晚上有
太多的Flamenco
都不妨我看到
眼前還未完全
展開的色彩

我穿過婚紗
店的門廊
我知道
冷待我的不獨是
瞪着許多眼睛的
魚市場
還有吃吃笑的

Searching for a Bakery

The drowsy alley won't mind
If I turn a few more corners
This is what I know
The sunlight is not far off
Though the terrace has yet to show its face
Or nod at me knowingly
And no one on the street
Picks up a leaf
For no reason
To smile at the streetlamps overhead

All this I know
I know the city has too much
Fruit wine and tapas
Just like the night has
Too much flamenco
I might as well see
The colors before my eyes
Not yet in bloom

I pass through the doors
Of wedding shops
And I know
It's not just the fish market
Giving me the cold shoulder
With so many staring eyes
But also the chuckling

鮮花
我知道都不可吃
但在這早晨
誰知呢?

我知道
這只是此城
跟昨日一樣的日子
昨日我不知道
還要走多遠
才找到落腳的地方
一個陌生的地方
我知道
不會因一夜而熟悉
早上起來
也只能記認
昨夜的路
曾經迷失的路
好認了一點
就像這時
陽光灑進了一點
在似曾來過的地方
拐另一個彎
便能擁抱那滿滿
綻開的溫暖

這我都知道
在這早晨的背後
還有一個人在睡
昨夜的洗衣機
打開了圓門

Fresh flowers
I know I can't eat
But on this morning
Who knows?

I know
In this city
Today is just like yesterday
Yesterday I didn't know
How far I'd have to walk
Until I found a place to crash
I know
A foreign place
Will not become familiar overnight
Waking up in the morning
I can only recognize
The street from last night
And the street where I lost my way
Is now easier to identify
Like how right now
The sun's rays approach
Turning another corner
On a once visited place
To embrace a fully
Blossoming warmth

All this I know
Behind this morning
Another person sleeps
The round door
Of last night's washing machine

未關
被逼早起的咖啡壺
正打着呵欠
等我回來

Is not yet shut
And the coffee pot woken up early
Starts yawning
Awaiting my return

當我再看見河的時候

當我再看見河的時候
它已消失了許多年

沿著水泥河堤走下去
寬闊的河床停著狹長的河身

那是一管沉默的筆
不再描摹水的洪大

魚的死亡，蛇的凝睇
揮動的臂與掙扎的腿

堤上的村莊早吃飽莊稼
蹲在內庭消化了許多年

巴士站與公路牌一直巴望
無聊才玩起繁殖的遊戲

河需要歡好聲嗎
水原是沒意見的

像我們拋下鏽蝕的鉤
釣著流水和行雲

不再積聚甚麼了
雷打了雨卻下不來

By the Time I Saw the River Again

by the time I saw the river again
it had been gone for many years

walking along the cement embankment
the wide riverbed lays along the river's slender body

a silent pen
no longer tracing the river

the death of fish, the staring snakes
flailing arms and struggling legs

the village on the bank has long ago eaten its crops
squatting at home digesting for years

bus stops and road signs are always looking
playing proliferation games when bored

does the river need lovemaking
the water has nothing to say

like the rusty hooks we cast away
to catch running water and passing clouds

nothing gathers anymore
thunder strikes but the rain won't fall

我們在河床上曬太陽
晾衣，工作和休息

一步便跨過去
總忘了影子

像一管筆在身後暗瘂
幸福的日子不寫甚麼

on the riverbed we bask in the sun
hang up clothes, work, and rest

in a single step we cross over
always forgetting our shadow

streaming behind us like a mute pen
on lucky days, there's nothing to write

燈籠

中秋前一天忽然想到做一個紙紮燈籠
我問別人可在甚麼地方買到竹篾呢
誰知下了班又循著原路回去
傭懶的身軀靠在巴士上層的窗沿
疲倦是天上找不到的月亮
還是我隱隱收藏的藉口？

中秋前一夜如常在餐桌前看兒女的功課
湯裏撈出來淡淡的白肉點了醬油停在口腔
讓控制著情緒的話語容有空間消化回轉
一份功課看完又遞來另一份，嘗試解說
讓舌尖把黏著的臢肉筋脈剔離骨頭的關節
卻隨夜氣與電視聲響的相混而囁嚅起來

中秋前一天我在想我到底要甚麼呢
月餅太油膩風琴摺燈籠不安全
燈泡塑料燈籠要甚麼便有甚麼了
還有月亮你要看也不難看到
兒女要買螢光棒似還有妥協的餘地
都甚麼年代了你要擔心事情還多著呢

中秋前一夜我又在沙發上陷下來
兒子在超載的書包與儲物櫃之間來回
隔斷熒屏的一瞬我驚覺煩躁又在莫名累積
女兒忽然惶恐地叫那邊有飛蟲
她老是忘了蛾的名字今夜又一次糾正
虛指玻璃上的灰影卻發現底下一隻淡綠色的蛾

Lanterns

The day before Mid-autumn, I suddenly think to make paper lanterns
I ask around for where I can find bamboo strips
But who knew that after work, I'd follow the same road home again
My weary body leaning against the top window of a double-decker bus
Is fatigue the moon we cannot find
Or my dimly hidden excuse?

The night before Mid-autumn, I look over my son and daughter's homework
Pork ladled from soup and dipped into sauce catches in my mouth
To give the words that manage emotions space to digest and turn back
One worksheet follows another with attempts to explain
To let the tip of my tongue pick out the leftover tendons from bones
But along with the mingling of night air and TV sounds, I begin to stammer

The day before Mid-autumn, I wonder what on earth I truly want
Mooncakes are too greasy, cellophane lanterns unsafe
Light bulbs, plastic lanterns—whatever you want
Even the moon won't be hard to see, if you try
The children ask for glowsticks, as if there's still room for compromise
Look at the century we're in, your many worries await

The night before Mid-autumn, I sink back into the sofa
My son shuttles between his stuffed schoolbag and shelf
I am startled awake by the flashing TV screen, annoyed for no reason
My daughter suddenly cries out in fright, there's a flying insect
She always forgets it's called a moth and is corrected once again
I gesture to the grey shadow on the glass yet find a pale green moth below

中秋前一天我買來了棉紙和竹篾
還有小時候用過，油光半透的包書紙
我紮好一隻昆蟲的骨架，兒女便從功課中
站了起來，幫忙把彩紙一片一片糊上
虛空的地方。我們微笑著起飛了
在月亮還未出來時碰到了月亮

The day before Mid-autumn, I buy cotton paper, bamboo strips,
And with the glossy, plastic film I used for binding books as a child
Fashion the frame of an insect, and the children
Rise from their homework to help glue pieces of colored paper
Over empty spaces. Smiling, we fly,
Meeting the moon before the moon arrives

到了這個時候仍在寫詩

到了這個時候，寫詩
是不是輕易了點，譬如
望向窗外，望著開著的木棉
隨暮色暗下來，會不會
輕易找到不那麼陳套
雖然未必一定有意思的
意象，或光是白描
白描也有自己走慣了的路
會不會在那隱晦的角落
突然拐彎，轉到自己也不知道
的地方？就像那海港
這時在我張開的瞳孔裏
有了點輪廓，但細節
大多時候敵不過
隱喻。我常想像的一艘渡輪
此際正在黑暗中航行
像我在發展中的句行，如今
停歇在山邊一個小亭裏
我可以想像
賣豆腐花的木桶
我可以撫摩
雞公碗崩缺的邊緣
但我還是怯於
那種如雷的吆喝：
今時今日
你還在做夢
現實是不是我的詩
輕易跌在發泡膠盒裏

To Still Write Poetry

Hasn't writing poetry
Become simpler? Like
Looking out the window at the red cotton tree
Fading with twilight, will it be
Simpler to find less proverbial
Although surely meaningful
Images, or just sketches?
Even a sketch follows a common path
Will it suddenly turn at that
Ambiguous corner, entering a place
It doesn't know, like how the harbor
Inside my enlarged pupil
Has somehow taken form? But details
Are often no match for
Metaphor. A ferry I frequently picture
Is now sailing in the dark
Like the lines I develop. These days
Stopping in a pavilion by the hill
I can imagine
The douhua for sale in a wooden bucket,
I can caress
The ruined rims of the rooster bowls,
Yet I am still afraid of
Those thundering cries:
Here and now
You are still dreaming.
Is the present moment my poems
Easily falling inside styrofoam boxes

蓋上必要的蓋
或加上油條
在我的詩的
骨節裏？

到了這個時候，寫詩
或許已變得輕易
多了，譬如望向窗外
此際我真的望向窗外
黑暗中只餘維園
暗淡的燈，還有沒有花節
還會不會換上
新的妝容，新的
卻依然漫長卻依然不大深刻的
詩句？但又有甚麼
相干呢，到了這個時候
當別人已經走了
當明天就是清明
不是登高，不是
掃墓，就是那麼
那麼理所當然的
寫詩

Closing the lids that need to be closed
Or adding youtiao
To the joints
Of my poems?

At this time, writing poetry
Has perhaps become much
Simpler, for instance looking out the window
Right now I am in fact looking out the window
Only Victoria Park's lights glow dimly
In the darkness, will there still be a flower festival
Will they put on
New makeup, new
Yet ever long and ever not-so-deep
Stanzas? But what does that have to do
With anything? Now,
When others have already left
When tomorrow is Qingming
If we don't go climbing, or
Tomb sweeping, then there may be
Nothing left to do
But to write poetry

Acknowledgments

To Mom and Dad, who gave me a bilingual education and encouraged my love of reading—thank you, this book would not exist without you and your immeasurable support. Mom, especially—you know you are often the very first reader of my drafts! Cynthia, Henry, and Kevin, thank you for being my cheerleaders and for sharing words of affirmation when I needed them most.

I found my calling as a literary translator in college, and for that I am grateful to Annie Janusch, who led my very first translation workshop, and the translation teachers who have guided me along this journey: Jennifer Scappettone, Haun Saussy, Lynn Xu, and Jason Grunebaum. I'd be remiss to not give a special shout-out to the members of the Third Coast Translators Collective (TCTC), who read some of these poems in their early stages and created a sense of community that made translating feel like the opposite of lonely.

I am also grateful to the American Literary Translators Association (ALTA) for having a direct hand in the publication of this book: the Emerging Translator Mentorship Program provided me with the funds and platform to work on this book and publish early versions of these poems, creating valuable exposure for both myself and Derek. Through ALTA, I also had the great fortune of being mentored by Jennifer Feeley, who workshopped many of these poems and remains a mentor to this day: Jennifer, your advice, friendship, and wisdom have been a guiding light. To everyone who has answered my translation or publishing-related questions over the years: Chenxin Jiang, Andrea Lingenfelter, Jenna Tang, Jeremy Tiang, Kelsi Vanada, Alex Zucker, thank you!

Many thanks are also in order to Cris Mattison and the folks at Zephyr Press for putting such a beautiful book together. Cris, your patience and thoughtful edits made this book better. Thank you for fielding my hundreds of emails. Tammy Ho, thank you for championing Hong Kong literature and me and Derek's work, and for being the first person to publish my poetry in *Cha*. Rita, thank you for contributing your original drawing of a cha chaan teng to grace the cover of this book.

Finally, I truly believe I would not have become a translator if not for Derek Chung, whose poems showed me a new side of the city I grew up in and gave me a reason to translate. Derek—you put trust in me when I was still a college student to translate your work. Thank you for your guidance, support, and for "getting it" when it comes to translation. This book has been a long time coming, and we did it. I'm lucky to call you not just the author I translate, but a true collaborator.

Previous versions of these poems appeared in the following publications:

Exchanges: Journal of Literary Translation (December 2018): "In the Rain Stands a Bright House"; "Mosquitoes"
Circumference (Fall 2020): "Housework"
World Literature Today (June 2021): "Festival"
The Common (June 2021): "The Cha Chaan Teng on Fortune Street"; "A Cha Chaan Teng That Does Not Exist"
Voice & Verse Poetry Magazine (Issue 70): "Bowrington Bridge"; "1 : 25000"; "Pineapple Bun"; "Searching for a Bakery"

Contributors

DEREK CHUNG (鍾國強) is an acclaimed poet, essayist, novelist, translator, and critic from Hong Kong. The author of eight poetry collections, three essay anthologies, two short story collections, and two books of poetry criticism, he is known for turning his gaze towards everyday objects and writing poems that weave personal history with broader societal themes. He is also a literary translator, having translated Charles Simic, Li-Young Lee, Williams Carlos Williams, W.S. Merwin, Carl Sandburg, and others into Chinese. Notable works include *The Growing House* (2004), *Umbrellas that Blossom on the Road* (2015), *In the Rain Stands a Bright House* (2018), and *The Lives of Animals* (2023).

Chung is a two-time winner of the Youth Literary Awards and five-time winner of the Hong Kong Biennial Awards for Chinese Literature, among other accolades. In 2019, he was a featured poet at the International Poetry Nights in Hong Kong (IPNHK), one of the most influential international poetry event series in Asia. He has been named Artist of the Year (Literary Arts) by the Hong Kong Arts Development Awards. His work has been translated into English and Japanese, and published widely in Hong Kong and internationally. You can find him at Patreon at @growing2houses.

MAY HUANG (黃鴻霙) is a writer and translator from Hong Kong and Taiwan. Her translations of Chinese literature have appeared in *The Common*, *World Literature Today*, *Circumference*, *Exchanges*, *The Massachusetts Review*, *Washington Square Review*, *Books From Taiwan*, and elsewhere. Writers she has translated into English include 鍾國強 Derek Chung, 璇筠 Leung She-Kwan, 邱常婷 Chiou Charng-Ting, and 盧勁馳 Clayton Lo.

Huang graduated from the University of Chicago with honors in 2019. She was awarded ALTA's 2020 Emerging Translators Mentorship Program to translate Derek Chung's work, and in 2022 she received a PEN/HEIM grant to translate Chiou Charng-Ting's *Young Gods*. Based in Berkeley, you can find her on Twitter at @mayhuangwrites.

With her beautiful translation and illuminating introduction, May Huang brings us inside the world of Derek Chung, a world that is palpably personal and at the same time universal. Chung's nuanced representation of the texture and ambiance of life in the "Fragrant Harbor" is unique.

— *Michelle Yeh, Distinguished Professor of Chinese, UC Davis*

From the sharp edge of a can, the subtropical air laden with mosquitos, to a mother's day filled with housework, these poems reveal everyday epiphanies and complex emotions with wonderful precision, wit, and a deep affirmation of love and life. May Huang's translation of Derek Chung's poetry establishes a deeply-rooted understanding of the poetics, culture, and emotions conveyed in the works of the prominent Hong Kong poet.

— *Jennifer Wong, author of* 回家 Letters Home *(Nine Arches Press)*

POETRY $16

ISBN-13: 978-1938890284

51600

9 781938 890284

ZEPHYRPRESS.ORG